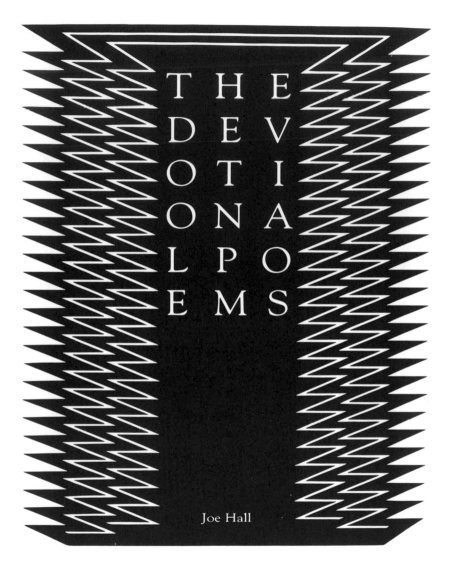

THE DEVOTIONAL POEMS

Joe Hall

The Devotional Poems
by Joe Hall

Black Ocean
Boston - New York - Chicago

Black Ocean
P.O. Box 52030
Boston, MA 02205
blackocean.org

ISBN 978-1-939568-01-4

Library of Congress Cataloging-in-Publication Data

Hall, Joe, 1982-
  [Poems. Selections]
  The devotional poems / Joe Hall.
      pages cm
  ISBN 978-1-939568-01-4
  I. Title.
  PS3608.A547265D48 2013
  811'.6—dc23
                        2013000484

FIRST EDITION

ACKNOWLEDGEMENTS

Thanks to the editors of the following journals for accepting versions of poems in this book: *1913, The Boog Portable Reader, Gulf Coast, HTML Giant, Lo Ball, No Tell Motel, Phoebe,* and *So & So.* "Post Nativity" was published as a chapbook by Publishing Genius in 2012. Thanks to Adam Robinson and Chris Toll.

Additional thanks to all those editors, large and small, unwitting and not: Jason Labbe, Christian Gerard, Kim Calder, J. Michael Martinez, Moriah Purdy, Brandon Shimoda, Danika Stegeman, and Robb St. Lawrence. Thanks to friends who helped me through everything else: Kyle McCord, Alec Muller, Mike Scalise, Tom Weaver, and, above all, Cheryl.

Thanks, finally, to the Black Ocean crew and the staff of the Santa Fe Art Institute.

CONTENTS

TRAILER PARK

Trailer Park

In an algorithm of trees exploding in your face, shaved from soap
in a prison cell, in a pair of yellow finches
alighting from high power lines over all these dudes
lying on their beds, palming their cocks, waiting for me
leached from circuits in a baroque array of evolving graphical
representations of a black economy, cancer, subverting process,
O Beast! O Christ!
in the mother fucking sound and mother fucking light
the iterations of thunder, the bass so high
it hurls you into the grass, Beast!
Only imminent, you cannot be found, waiting to subsume, fuck up
them cities, bring murder into the bridal chamber
and force armies to copulate in the killing field mud
Delete all images of yourself, crash this party, sink this continent
To petrify latitudes of soy and corn
to perform plastic surgery on everyone
beating to death the letter B while the rest of the alphabet watches
in a berserk horizon scouring clarity, Christ!
I will wait until I am the viscous core of three huge spinning heads
ten wasps in a monitor, a sweating cradle of fat
a bursting parabola of orange-yellow cubes called flowers
ten thousand livers whiffled like flutes secreting
shrines in dissolvable capsules
I will wait until I am an iron rake with a broken tooth biting
through the throat of this soil
I will not break down my tent
I will not follow a sign
I will wait until I am a singing corpse
being dragged across this landscape—O Beast! O Christ!
You are a lamb

Our Lady of Perpetual Devotion

You are about to select a kernel from a heap
of broken kernels on the gray perimeter
of a corn syrup plant; I am firing someone's dad's
25 into the dusk in what will be
a field of wheat next spring—BLAM—for
the hell of it—BLAM BLAM—Inside the cottage
Colby's birddog hunches like he has to crap
but doesn't; he's just shivering
In the main block: ladders oxidizing
smokestacks of burning seed
What can't be sacrificed?
What can't be divided?
Your hand reaches to stroke my neck
I aim the 25 at a bottle
and I tremble—Mary
Animal
where is your altar?

Gasoline Chainsaw Jesus

Pushing through cornstalks, the rows, this same-y apocalypse
soiling itself in the sterile spotlight of the moon, this burning
Snatching blisters of pseudoephedrine
lights turning on, pressing a lit joint into the couch skirt
The vacuum hum running
over lists of what needs doing, blasts searing a tree line or cinema carpet
the Harmenz of heaven, of broken things
things thrown away
or ovens—wet prairie grass between
my fingers, my hands, between this loam
grown unable to support basic algorithms, this third field
looking after each row for real shade
Your name does not
appear—O Beast! O Christ! Zombie
rapture thing, survivors cling
to hell, Nazareth, what needs repair, what you
seat beside you is not a body, like copper
ripped through walls, flowers made of
Blah blah blah, what you salvage
is a mobile of nerves on an electrified wire
writhing in the ecstasy of
Trees don't understand sin—a column of expanding fire
pushing through mounds of sassafras and rising insects
so why sit in your accelerator's ring
under rusting constellations on long ruined axes giving
smashed particles a name? Lord Jesu
Thou Didst bow Thy dying head
Upon the tree, this not a prayer without your
Following O be not now / More
Dead to me! Word
without which—My bowels released in a blackout

in the land of doors, O Beast!
Christ! Where is your profile?
I can't find you
in this field of pixels, these words made in China
this bleached and parceled
wilderness, heart-muscle
drifting crops of orange tissue
Lead me into the heat of your terrible body
Give me shelter
or tell me where to find enough blood
to turn back this fire

Weaker Leg

In all this waiting to be saved
The back bone splits

The dark jelly speaks
Into the canal, the difficult water

Divides in your swarm, your golden
Electricity seizes, hip to toe

Eating, joining heavy metals
Radiation of flesh, node inflating

To spore the wind, the surface of the socket
The femur's chipped ball turns roughly around and into

The bulldozer mixing black walnuts and slave graves
Tissue tightening, marsh that tears

Drowns in a fire gripped and singing
By you, a churning murderous tree

Nativity

And in the jungle of my youth where I imagine a body as sleek as an eel's
even there a head rolls along what seems to be the boundary
of my yard, the head that feeds on fingernails and
idiotic worries, some part of it bleeding, maybe its
mouth, some part of it laughing, maybe
its eyes, and the head just rolls—And here the manger is
the Christ baby, his bones a dense web of revised saints
and household motherfuckers—Still, I look back, feeling
the superheated wind on my shoulders amid a panoply
of lights, some holy spirit lurking in the eaves
a perverse, crystal man-o'-war, a spinning
zoetrope above a bratty shepherd squeezing puss
from a zit while a great burden is let loose
between the virgin's thighs—One magician sees fire
racing star to star, another magician sees the infant image
repeated on the brass censer he holds and looks back to
the manger where there are a thousand Christs now
bawling in the ampitheatrical barn, commanding him in voices
like tiny bells to whittle Christs from cork to be set adrift
on an alkaline sea, while living out his life
in a caravan's most wretched tent,
and the final magician can't believe he came all this way with no one
to suck off—The scene piles upon the scene
as I look for the original cell
in a mansion of unspooled film
in each transparency's absolute weight
its own burning, ruining self—Return
to scene: desert, night on the Nazareth road
sound of boots scraping macadam, icy fists of stars
and the armored vehicles' bricky glow

Grief

Hoop of pollen, comb of stamen
Honeysuckle: iron

Path as thread as bow
Not as molten as weeping pores goes

I did not mean to complain
Scrabble of root fiber blown from soil

Where if I find a chunk of hive
Light and empty as a flute

Where if I kiss the corpse's lips
Give my breath to that stillness

If *should all the World so wide to atoms fall*
Should the Aire be shred to motes

If for a moment you do not decay
And shake your casket singing

Come Our Lady Before Our Lord

If this is weeping, it isn't—It's
the shattered mouth of a flooded subway
It's bees iced in their hives, a crocus' spears
shaking from soil—goodnight
Goodnight, I love you, I love you too
Ok, sleep well—it's the man who draws maps
of non-existent continents, naming capitals
after corrupt and dead popes or linebackers
from the twilight of his second favorite football team
It's a web page of clumsy pornography
waiting for its very first hit—
Svmer is icumen in, sing cuccu, I miss you
goddammit, you're like an actor with a gorilla head,
an elephant head, and all the animal heads
There's no need to go to the zoo, because I'm
already walking on all fours to give it
a name, to give it anything I know
This isn't weeping, but it has the same rhythm

Passenger

Now that I'm here
In heavy engines

Margin gathering what falls
Runs along the discs dragged

Through the bowls, through the vermin
Suckers and long burdock

And the wind lifted
All the things around me

Receipts and soft packs, a rind
Of coffee spoken onto a plastic lid

Some slipped, thorn by thorn
From the window—I was speeding

Because I don't know
The embankment

They could not follow
Over streams, softening logs

Through two banks
Of bulletproof glass

Seams of clover around the vacants
House after house until the row ends

Tasseled spike after spike until the row ends

That gathers all the world

Caught on razor wire
Jewel, redeemer, blister of sweetness

Utter trash
If you will part these thorns

If you will bend

Post Nativity

It's true I took courage following the new star, passing visored old women
Lounging with long cigarettes in the high seats of steamrollers
Churning on empty, keeping pace with donkey carts
Pulled by gangs of men in orange jumpsuits
Bags tied over their heads, keeping pace with a falcon turning regular circles
Around an evil sun—I watched the flame clothe a tree

A staircase led down to where the stump should be
With a football, a stethoscope, and a quarter ounce, I watched men
Steer that broke-down Chrysler into the cut, but the star
Kept shifting, the channel kept changing, we were dancing
In a field of chest-high yarrow with Floridian blondes
In wet t-shirts and thongs and dudes with stomachs
Like six lacquered doorknobs

I brushed aside the pale saucers of blossoms
To shoot my piece at the unadvertisable colors
Of the hurtling sky, I climbed into a pickup truck bed and we tore off
The crickets' work rising: mezzo piano to way too fucking
Loud—that was back when I'd wake up with a sumac branch for a leg
Or I'd have a salamander's head and a toad for a tongue, when I was
Puking behind the hot tub in the sand and winter grass

I could make out bits of bun and meat, and he was on the deck
Painting glitter on the loose putty of his dick
He was laughing, calling me a cunt, a bitch, a whore—I could smell the sea
The stars were switching places, the traders' stalls were
Caked with sandy mud, I was weeping or laughing
I couldn't tell the difference—O Beast, O Christ—I was following you
Down the stone stairs under weird smoldering lamps
Of red moss where you asked me to take my clothes off and I did

We proceeded into the surgical theater where technicians were performing
Autopsies on beheaded semicelebrities, their bodies' insides
Bright as candles, I felt I was packed full
Of car fresheners and hibiscus flowers
Someone raised a freshly detached heart in his fist

You climbed into my lap or I wake up and my balls are dragging behind me
Like wet paper bags of trash, or how did I get this old?
Why am I sitting in a stale bathrobe trying
To rub feeling back into my fingers? Am I a dictator on a
Throne of sugar in a castle of cake? Night eats this place, or I wake
And have to sling my dick across my shoulders
Like a lamb—O Beast, O Christ—sleeping in a huge kiln

On a plain of upset bricks, static television screen, a flat emergency
Tone then the warnings of an angular language, a government webpage's
DOS-like green letters on a watermelon wallpaper—hush
Hush now under the billboards of incinerated continents, heaps of smaller
Textured things on heaps of larger, less textured things, looking for you
In the dirt baked to a library of hexagonal tiles where the wind picks up
A scarf of dust near a giant thorn of a tree, wrestling
With random arms and hands in the ash
The night sky gone berserk with light—O Beast, O Christ

Can you rise through perforated body armor, salt, and shale?
Can you rise through a substrate of fractured monitors, bone shards
Charred engine blocks, chipped motherboards, pottery pieces
Through LOLOMG, *Dear Dave it's been a hard couple weeks*
And Free 14 Year Olds Fucking! Can you split
The hull of human information—are you the continental Nazareth?
Are you the pores of a land
That is over the word virgin? Are you the land?
I suggest suitcase number 8

I suggest the NSF grant funded study of a hecatomb of scientists
Casting my vote through an astrolabe of petrified eyes, I thought
I saw you, I thought I saw you down in the cut, I thought I saw your face

Behind the fire, the spinning thaumatrope, one of
The discs is my god; my god, why dost thou part from me? And
The other is, again, I want to be your cell, your lens, onion
Skin, a terminal enveloped in your electricity, your boiler, a router, a
Synapse—I can't stop thinking about this shrapnel, please
Make me your mug, your pipe, your ashtray

After the party, you wrote on my face
Make me your flute, your needle, the chamber for your cartridge
You poured beer in my ear, took pictures, stripped me
Make me your drum, your bell, your trampoline
You made me walk on my knees on concrete, urinated on me
Took pictures (thumbs up!), dragged me by my handcuffs down the hall

Make me your pen, your two turntables and a microphone
Your air raid siren, your silence, the IED
Detonated, my brain slammed against my skull—O Beast, O Christ—
Make me your staff, your sword, your brick, your bottle, your rod
You stacked me in a pile of other bodies, you took pictures
Now here I am in a grocery store trying to remember my name
Because when a bird gets his head cut off, he dances
Not because he is happy but because he is dead

You're a Falcon, like he said, a falcon, but Christ
Beast, I am a prison and you are
Screaming, beating against the bars, both
Inside and out, you are two falcons
One circling the sun at its zenith, one
Inside, one out, both screaming
Both beating against the bars

THE ABYSS HAS NINE NAMES
AND I HAVE SHOWN YOU
THREE

How it was the stone died

While the eye intervenes between
nerve and bone, shaves and
planes, building a ghost from
a body, his hand behind the saw
as ribs unfurl like cardinal wings, a factory
fills my voice—Disembody, offer
an alternative totalitarian system
know not even nothing perfectly
and steal from me me me me me

Ventricle

wind flutes

stone *wind*

Stone wound

I want to touch you with the rough tombs of your fathers
with the wild flowering blood and wire
or a pear, rotting fish, almonds, the dock breeze
blown pixilation, thickets the eye eats
A trail of light carrying itself
through walls, false walls, years as trance
where one may speak once
One may drink twice from the cup
at the central door
the end of one's life
the completion of this bracket
this scaffold to restrain

Wind—
yoked to plough

through rooms patience moves
and inherits

no real ground

I believe in the Cowboys, the Yankees, and the Holy Ghost
I belong to the father, the son
Through this logo I deny the devil in Christ, God
Behind a heavy door, I etch myself in the image
of you on a promontory, a recluse collecting records
of the shape of the world, where we walk hand in hand
in a field of heather, letters scrolling up out
of theater darkness, taking turns on a one hitter
getting loose, kind of stupid

Of this long memory
of fire hung from venting fissures

On an axis, a spear is two stars piercing
a piece of carbon paper Eucharist

on some other tongue
or stance of poverty eroded

into want and sickness

Fog, this cold wind frames
what cross beam collects
Breath against like glass

Iron swinging, censer
little thin, Little tin
tick, tock

Who can I love?

The codeless tundra trembles
this unloved train of assholes
Turning a marble slab into a cone of powder
These dollars I got, cousin of pity
it ain't happening like you said it would
Current through hard smoke
the slow drifting ashes
during the blackout stillness
I could only imagine you
moving, modeled to move
pulled from your tissue
half a continent waiting in darkness

Were you a window or sugar
blown into skin?

I never call you
my bitch or even my boo—I pray
I rest my head upon this tree
and watch a cup dwindling in a field
a holy book like a wounded star
throwing off an arm of annihilating fire
a scent of clean clothes
and sex discolored by unremitting light
I worked so hard to live
in an altar that could be your expanding
lung, I thought, an observatory for zeroes
and occluded by some

Watching the stone's eye
open—shovel cutting

leaf mold drifts randomly
generating cemetery

randomly generating
Cemetery, faltering

Over shapes the tongue can't make—Roof

Soft gate

Just say my name, and I will be with you

How it is the stone dies

Entanglement Seal

Where your forms are bent and bent
Into a coil that is you, the shape

Overpassing describes—a comb, spring onion
Mosquitoes breeding in a Big Gulp

What collects in the cut, the small moving
Is still slowed, slows

This in that: clot or cable
Another effervescence

You are shit, I have implied
Or in shit, bubbling

Through a final irradiation
Mushroom, exile

Strange and soft to touch
Some days I think

Of course you've retreated

Slush Altar

What is a lamb, Christ?
Do you take from slaughter?
Is what you want to regard
debased by a system of yourself?
I try to follow this thing rising through crushed time

tilting into soil, its shape lost, material changing
a toothpick crane astride a crane on fire
the unlike-me-guy voted from the reality polis
by carrion birds with crazy genitals

They don't like riddles and mystifiers
those scientists who nailed you down
You gripped the burning buzzers in each wrist
Pilate straightened his tie and asked
Is that your final answer?

Of Smoke, the Architecture of a Tree

Denser than a star folding into itself, bringing
to my body what I can know—If between two witnesses
distance is the only objective phenomena
and aging is a physical experiment
each person performs alone

Duh, I'll die
while we accelerate toward the margins
of the universe, a particle of thought, growing
younger, sitting on a powder blue stool
eating Mary Lou's donuts
asses flapping in the breeze
unable to grind or contemplate or weep
unable to add or subtract to preserve these slender brackets

writing themselves down in the theater of air
an allowance of space where blood rusts
in the derelict warehouse's silence
a field, a bone fragment, a stone, Christ
Mr. Bumpy Fruit
Mr. Waste Land
Let's Call It Fallow
Dull tool stripping the screw?

O little error script
little twisted limb

Our Lady of Ash Wednesday

A third virgin carved from horn and
this horn slowly beginning to branch
upward into the night like sad
quiet lightning? Mary, Saint, morning, noon
and eve, you yet conceive
the soil on which afterbirths are flung
with what is pulled between her legs
her thighs and his hands and
your hands and my body
before the livestock's impassive eyes
Splinter of terror, splinter of awe—Mary, Saint
Shake me useless

2 EXORCISMS

I Was Living in a Boarded Up House Without Heat. I Was Still Sick and had Unpaid Medical Bills. The Record He Gave Me Was GOOD OLD COUNTRY GOSPEL

Cutting pills in half with a long knife
lying here, Christ, between the wet and breathing purple walls
not a mouth of a lantern or candle at a desk in the basement
office struggling to complete disability paper work that says basically
saltwater guttering in forever, watching a mirror where my fiancé
towels herself, listening
while something giant swims through the night
waking up medicated again and whacked off
thinking about two pregnant people bonking in old snow
hurrying to gray water, locating herbs that breathe
under the leaves—The gunshot still not finding the fox
on the embankment opposite this house where in sunlight
on the cutting board, royal masses of brain sit
splashed in flour—Spike, wrist, noose, tree, hanging weight
soldier lifting the blood corroded
by air on several hills, the small blue bells
of rosemary catching the first
rain, the wind blowing, the cold wind
blowing, let it through—that's beautiful
in theory—You are all these things, in theory
if everything is married—The continued weeping—the nerves
crushed by fractured vertebrae as the wind flexes
the fine cedar branches before or after
lying in bed reading, sick again
Don't tell me beauty is symmetrical
it's a man with multiple eyes married
to a woman with the quills of a porcupine
it's the lamb warped into a skinny feral dog
with blue-pink forelegs, paws, beautiful goat

guilty of conspiring against the lion, screwing his head
between the prison house bars, an iteration of a green-blue Jesus
gripped by decay, emerging from a sepulcher
that looks like a punched in hive or
the toothy mouth of a beast so
huge the page can't contain it—Nope, not
quite, it can't be seen
held—it's a force, a wind, a ravaging
sustaining—Christ, how close are you to this?
Everything soft, everything bleached under
brush giving way to rain, the compost smell, rendering
petals, rendering not the sun
but coronas on an imaginary lens, rendering
wind, the I wants and I'm weaks, the I did
file the hill into a screw and the tree
into a swan's neck, magnitude of
raining hard, I laid down by the window and felt such
sweetness, rendering
why and to what or who—such weight
crushes, deranges—knowing
this pleasure will end then, my hands
numb way after I woke to daylight: prayer
a specific weight—it was a party
everyone was there
like the appearance of dwindling
like it all started in a mine shaft
this pleasure—this deer print
in the spillway's frozen mud
this interval, the moment you pass
through a sieve
one arm sunk into weakness
we grip, as if both slipping
and work our bodies into
each other, this flood

making naked the slope
taking the soil, the sweetness
this woman, her brain uncasing my body
lying down in the clover stream, a child
got beefy enough to punch, wailing
through my abdomen—wondering
if people see a wrecked socket or just a night watchman at the mall
copper wire ripped through
the walls or trees playing video games
all perverse screaming leaves
peeled apart like cards
in a deck, faces framed in a dead acre of unknown space
collecting white electric dust, outmoded
obsolete, angry all the time—I'm these things, let me also be
your platform, your wind spore, the warmth, Christ
let me be a camera and you the virgin contestant, the dead and the soil
let me be the feeling in your fingers, because I am losing mine
Don't let me slide into paralysis
I'll write you more letters, Christ, I will this time
I'll be good if my hands don't die—Onion grass
and mud, the steer skeleton chipped into meal
the kudzu and rose, chickory, pokeweed
mayapple—Don't paralyze me
I'll be the flattened opossum, the steaming
swatch of maggots dissolving a deer
chicken shit flooding into the sea
Don't let me slide into paralysis, I'll be
rolled into a giant missile, the gore forced through
a whale's spout, in an industrial dehydrator
the pond of clotting blood sprinkled around
tulips to keep them from being eaten, air in the pneumatic punch
creek violet, all improbable wildflowers, particulate
matter in the miners' lungs and the dust on the needle
descending on your father's vinyl, that song you

needed to hear to sleep under
one face of the devil—Death
looked like the self in the mirror, growing
like a dilating eye, I know I am fat melted for dogs
vats of brown and purple reconstituted muscle
at your hand, eating blades of grass, lilies
and nematodes, opera houses of mandibles
and frozen ferns, various intersections of
filth, light, the way things move—tangled hair
substrates of shaved, slaughtered neverminds, I am
laughing as the exploded globe
of your expanding integers falls like—We do not
murder that huge ball of pink grasping
hands that turns what it grasps into a new, further, grasping
hand expanding the radius from the center, time
coiled at our feet like a mean rope of neon feces—Is there a way
to convince you I mean what I'm saying?
Spring, last frost on the prairie grass, a friend leaning
in his doorway eating an apple, waiting
for whatever, because if you remove the venom
you kill the man, or all crucifixions
made of cake and fruit, not to mention pleasure or the RZA
If you are dust drifting through light
not what's lost, what you lose, moving slow this time
Chew the pill to taste the medicine
load of rivets—what
can be clutched, still soft
let it go like a tropical bird into the late Indiana spring
Tell me how to make things right, Christ
I've hurt some people, that's for sure, trying
a terrifying love though never mugged, fucked, or called out for it
crying between the rows of my leased garden, my good
arm broken, weeds choking the mustard
Tell me what's right—the horn in the leaves

the first wildflower of the season
pushing aside party streamers like fingers and tongues, waterfalls
of newspapers, and these words decay too
placed on your stone like a lettuce wreath
asking forgiveness for being stupid and weak
Forgive me for being stupid and weak
I will offer what is healed O Christ! O Beast!
Forgive me for asking to heal

Ghost Farm

In a punk garden
kissing gore

by burnt amaranth wands
and morning glories

Regain the tongue
cut from my spine

Regain the tongue
deep in the rock

"Even Iron Heals"

When they sing the voice rises shakes and rises
to the tones of the song, the wound
complains and shakes, it feels so
when the wound is looked at the looker
begins to when the light
source is raised the plant
climbs when the throat is
elongated the note sung when I
walked on thin margins of gray grass
and asphalt grit when he asked if someone
trespassed on his property at what point could he
kill her—I can't believe spring is here
or I pay to have my head filter radiation and who
owns the trucks and this equipment unloaded on
my lawn? And if it's a cliché to talk about small creatures
then we'll talk about the big creatures, the glory and devastation
the thyme 9/10ths dead and gone
only a few green stars left under the mulch
when you run out of trespasses
to be forgiven for when whatever is what gets us off
when the wind blows, standing by the window
with a new shoulder bag, two hours early
to interview for a job that's been liquidated
when you feel innocent, you feel innocent when
the wind blows, I spend
all weekend in bed, Lord I do—I
want you when the wind blows
let it blow the altar an opening
built from split and charred wood, stones
from incomplete circuits and algorithms growing
abortions made of petals, the altar prayer as movement through

between its scaled, black limbs or
a river, wading toward you through the not weak
current, to the center, the altar being to descend
beneath, to be there, among what
pulls hard and no air in the river or a hand
on my neck in a cold rain that erodes proposed
worlds like mud clods, like a cold rain that
erodes microcosm factories like
mud clods, a cold rain that
erodes economies of rain, this
would be shameless and quotidian, Lord
I would describe my father
but I've already squeezed a misty
pink noise from the soaked
oblong loaf of his lungs
I'd like to think you hate a lie told
twice, so forgive me
a screw made of soap
a violin case full of mucus, and here I am
standing between two scrub pines
drinking the river-fading glister
overhead, the honk of migrating once-was'es descending
to the surface where parallel
blots are widening into a sentimental family tableaux
This is where I stick my head in the liquid
fire of the sun and piss myself while
burning vistas multiply
I affix the electrodes to my throat
Look kindly on our needs in this pilgrimage
and increase the electricity and
push my face further into a pillow on the hotel bed
When will you marry me?
I made a hit for a low resolution gaming system
it was perceived one of my hand shadows was

raping the other, so I'm not
allowed to get my hands within 50 feet
of light—It's not funny, I know, Lord
this is preface, preamble
tapping the bottoms with my knees
All I have to say is—the dead
in this room, this city or trailer park, the negatives
of buildings, the thin aluminum or drywall dust
I am small, lies are glue, what
I want doesn't matter, you
can build with it, I have
I do—Is this my word
through a woven screen
before the validation apparatus? Hoping
this is lost between
relay stations as blood from
the body, out of circulation
drifting interminably through
and maybe some cellos and maybe
one grain of light in an atlas darkness
Now *that's* an edifice, an altar
black teeth chewing on a huge purple intestine
one hand with no nerves rotting
the other strong with love
The devil takes his, that part
of a heart's chamber, six fingers
a hemisphere of this skull
when the sun hits wrinkled glass
in a small room in the shadow of a bookcase
pulling the chest hairs
from the electrode glue, squeezing
my neck and shoulders
trying to find a vein to send electricity through
without insurance or a job

without pain killers, neck unable to hold the weight
of the head without a nauseous shiver
a month, a time to stop measuring
My body failed, my brain failed, stopped
cell phone clock, a torn abdomen—intervening hell, Lord
like a hatch on a zeppelin over the city
your gates are opening—This is when the fire rises
when like tongued weeds a channel of green fire pours
when where I am broken is circumscribed by green fire
when through the soil the bones of opossums, rabbits, and saints
rise to float on the green fire
when Mary, when Lord, when Christ, when Jesus, when Beast
when Holy, when Ghost, when salt, when harrow, when snow
the deer dancing on its hind legs in this cul de sac
rose petals fixed to her yellowing skull

THESE ARE DEVOTIONAL POEMS

Locating

I hear your mouth filling with
Your tongue, wind dragged

In your lips before a braid
Flushes, spilling

Without aspect
Arresting and silence

How can I address this
Thrum—which

Is my Mary, Christ, or Beast? You cannot
All enter me, my little body tells me

It cannot take that you are many
And changing, I seem to know but still

In one time of one place dwell
In one state clear and weep

One shrinking word
Waiting on tender feet

Will you encircle me?
Or are you here, without passage

Encircled? Listen:
Is this a passage

Between words? Your tongue moving
When all the horns do not blow

Or is this between two voids, passing?
Lord, are you the basin?

Our Lady Walks Along It

Mary, if you give me a dipper full of water
I'll be able to live, to plant pansies
in the plastic lids of CD spindles
to enliven the porch which stands witness
to a burning house, and the pansies turn
their blotched faces to the flames, and I forgive
the colony of aphids clinging
to the blossoms and the flies feeding
there, on the honeydew, that's
a name for aphid crap—Oh and
I have to remember you are only a water dipper
and it is best to look for me in the dried fish store
and if the dried fish store should burn down, well
I never meant to go, to flee, to leave you

Our Lady Understands

That the soul is a braid of mating snakes
And what are snakes? Madonna
Immaculate Heart of Mary, heroism
lies only in death. Hence, there is no need to inquire
into the martyr's previous life
That's Pope Pius IX. Subject line: *Moosic*
Subject line: (no subject). Subject line: *I miss you*
What's the soul? *Impossible Outcome*
A game piece's button head, a body
so broken it is unbreakable. Without orifice
I'd be so happy to speak to you

Our Lady of Supreme Happiness

In the theater my silver wrists divide into almond tree
branches. They flower. I leave, I can't remember
the movie. When I begin praying to you
Mary, you are an icon carved
from a yellow tusk, you become
a horn thickened by milk, then a garlic clove
When I finish praying
you are still here, a flame
ranging roof to roof, the scent
of burning almonds blossoms. To live
is to borrow, and if we borrow
to live, then all life must be
a heap of trash, so rejoice

Homes

Flocking power, resonance, pool—gliding
through, I have brought you a peach

And you move toward it, station by station
Post by toppled border post

What do words mean to you?
Should I have said Speech? I have brought you a peach

And, I, too, am moving toward you, who I believe
Through heavy, roving lights and what is almost

How the ocean smells—House by house
Basement to top floor then trailer

Though I do not know when we will meet
If everything you reside in is sundered

Every cinderblock and stone, every burdock, two footpaths
Crossing pines and fire lingering

If I am unfaithful, set loose, again and again
Fractured, that escalation

I'll be gone, you'll be gone
Every Tuesday

Every remember
You kissing me between the neck

And shoulder, resting there
Raises itself on and above, this contract

Those insects spilling from his mouth
We could still sleep last night

And those dreams I'd have of digging deeper
Into the earth, the caverns of clean, even minerals

Clinging—the neighborhood
The sewer pipes, mailbox, tap water

And electricity so much dark, piled olivine
Where you appear

In a hood of flames in the crown of a tree
Live power lines whipping around you

And my body in this sleeping bag moves closer to you
Lemon Balm, and you say in this tent

That on its legs that carry us aloft
After so much scrambling

It is right to kill
That which takes what holds us

Because that is us
And we are nothing but that

I think that is what you said
It is hard to understand

What fire is speaking

Our Lady of Ghost Farm 2

It's June and someone is stopping in an empty corridor
Of SR 26 to abandon a rust colored Christmas Tree
It's June and packed into my spine is a cache of pearls soft as slush
I am a registered sex offender and you are a public school
I abused your name the first time I said it—the building burned
and I can see the house in the ash
better than I can see the house, the sores in my mouth
and the sugar that stings right through
It's June and I could lay down in your soft arms
of road-side weeds on some holiday
wild onions sprouting from my titties

Sacrifice

Must be flocking, swarm
As when the comb tenders what it is

A dad will abandon under
A lead sphere its surface inconstant with the expansion

Or contraction of half discs, lenses superheated
Weight, what it is tempting to call the exit

Wreck, has this missed it? Mangle, flock
Landscapes of junk passed through

You and Maria unnamed? This seat of dirt
In hardening braids as if

The infrastructure could pass like film through a projector
As if so much traveling wasn't Drain-O searching

Deeper into the intestine, and I do not know—I know I should know
Touch something, this hand

Should hold its own feeling
If touched, is it even in portion

Our altar?
If who returns to watch or pray

Where is no altar?
The bars of a constellation drawn

That pearls with a familiar scent

That hand holding steady

You are the wind that turns
The other stars, flies or motes of dust

The pulse, crest, and retreat
Into the stone unfolding

END NOTES

Borrowings, mistranslations. One from a friend:
12 - "Post Nativity" – "When a bird gets his head cut off, he dances /
not because he is happy but because he is dead" via Melissa Tuckey. It
is a quote from an Abu Ghraib detainee.